Merriam-Webster's
ADVANCED LEARNER'S
ENGLISH DICTIONARY

Study Guide

Merriam-Webster, Incorporated
Springfield, Massachusetts, U.S.A.

A GENUINE MERRIAM-WEBSTER

The name *Webster* alone is no guarantee of excellence. It is used by a number of publishers and may serve mainly to mislead an unwary buyer.

Merriam-Webster™ is the name you should look for when you consider the purchase of dictionaries or other fine reference books. It carries the reputation of a company that has been publishing since 1831 and is your assurance of quality and authority.

ISBN: 978-0-87779-552-0

Editor: Mark A. Stevens
Contributors: C. Roger Davis, Neil S. Serven, Penny L. Couillard-Dix
Design: Loree Hany

Made in the United States of America
2345QW/T12111009

Contents

Introduction

Merriam-Webster's Advanced Learner's English Dictionary offers enormous possibilities as a teaching and learning tool. Perhaps no single volume anywhere contains a larger trove of knowledge about the language, and particularly about the English that is spoken and written in the United States.

The aim of this guide, which is designed for use by both the classroom teacher and the student outside of the classroom, is to familiarize the learner with all of the dictionary's remarkable resources, through exercises that require locating every kind of information that is contained in its pages.

Most of the guide is devoted to its Exercises section (pp. 1–43). Before assigning or attempting an exercise, the teacher or student should consult the Notes section (pp. 44–51) for information about the subject of that exercise. The Answer Key (pp. 52–60) contains not just answers but helpful comments for the student who may have failed to answer an exercise correctly.

All the exercises may be freely photocopied and handed out in the classroom. If all the students have their own copies of the guide, the teacher may ask them to tear out the appropriate perforated page or pages and put away the rest of the guide before beginning a test.

An entire curriculum could be designed around the *Learner's Dictionary,* and a learner could spend a lifetime working with it and not exhaust its rich resources. We hope that this guide will help thousands of learners discover how valuable these resources can be as they strive to attain a mastery of English.

ALPHABETICAL ORDER

In each column below, number the words (1, 2, 3, 4, 5) in the order that you would find them in the dictionary.

1. ___ e-book
    ___ ebony
    ___ -ed
    ___ E. coli
    ___ eco-

2. ___ GPS
    ___ go-to
    ___ grabby
    ___ grab bag
    ___ Gothic

3. ___ kid-glove
    ___ kick up
    ___ Kabuki
    ___ kick-start
    ___ kickoff

4. ___ Oct.
    ___ o'clock
    ___ OD
    ___ odd couple
    ___ octave

GUIDEWORDS

Each exercise below shows the guidewords from a single page. In each list below them, circle the words that you would *not* find on that page.

1. **actually • add**

    adamant   acute
    actual   acuity
    adapt   adder

2. **alpha and omega • alternating current**

    alternate   alphabet
    alternative   altar
    alpha   Alsatian

3. **area code • arithmetic**

    arena   argue
    aristocrat   arise
    arm   arid

MOST COMMON WORDS

1. **Which of the following words are among the most common?**

although	thorough
through	cough
dough	borough
tough	bough
slough	enough

2. **In the following paragraph (from the *Washington Post*), circle all the words that are *not* underlined in the dictionary. Treat any word with an *–ing, -ed,* or *–ly* ending as if it did not have the ending. For extra credit, identify an idiom in the paragraph.**

> Young adults have reading habits that often differ from those of other age groups, which are constantly changing. Although teenagers may not come into libraries as frequently as other age groups, they are still interested in reading. Sometimes, however, reading for fun takes a back seat to all the other things that teens have to deal with in their lives.

HOMOGRAPHS

A. **Look up the entries for each word in italic type below, and find the homograph that defines the word in the way it is used in the sentence. Write the homograph number in the spaces below.**

1. They waited until the day *after*. ____

2. *After* dinner we took a taxi to the theater. ____

3. She always left the building right *after* she finished teaching. ____

4. Rebels were taking up *arms* against the new government. ____

5. Each candidate had *armed* himself with new facts and figures. ____

6. The *arms* on this jacket are too tight. ____

7. He entered the house by the *back* door. ____

8. She left home at 19 for New York and never looked *back*. ____

9. The singer was *backed* by two guitarists and a drummer. ____

B. For each word in italics below, write the number of the homograph where each word's meaning is defined, and write the appropriate part of speech (for example, "3, adjective").

1. Don't forget to sign and *date* the application. _____

2. The rebels tried to *fan* the fires of revolution. _____

3. The surgeon was able to *graft* skin over the scar. _____

4. Oil prices reached a new *high* last winter. _____

5. He brought her a jar of raspberry *jam*. _____

6. She *lapped* the runner who was in second place. _____

7. Did you *mail* all the out-of-town invitations? _____

8. I hope to visit in the *near* future. _____

9. We go to the movies *once* or twice a month. _____

10. The office is just *past* the intersection. _____

COMPOUNDS

A. Complete these compound nouns.

1. dental _____ : a special thread that is used to clean between your teeth

2. little _____ : ordinary people who are not wealthy, famous, or powerful

3. backseat _____ : a passenger in a car who gives driving advice to the driver

4. breeding _____ : a place where animals go to breed

5. life of _____ : a happy and comfortable life with few problems

6. chain _____ : a series of events in which each event causes the next one

7. dance _____ : an area where people can dance inside a restaurant, club, hall, etc.

8. dish _____ : a cloth that is used for drying dishes

9. looker- _____ : a person who watches something

10. local _____ : the time in a particular part of the world

B. Complete these compound adjectives.

1. face-_____ : done to keep someone from looking foolish

2. fire-_____ : able to produce a stream of fire from the mouth

3. habit-_____ : causing a strong need to regularly have something or do something

4. horse-_____ : pulled by a horse or a group of horses

5. double-_____ : having two rows of buttons

6. low-_____ : not of good quality

7. machine-_____ : in a form that can be used and understood by a computer

8. middle-_____ : relating to people about 40 to 60 years old

9. nerve-_____ : causing a person to feel very nervous

10. old-_____ : of or relating to the past

C. Many of the compounds below are written incorrectly. Write the correct form in the blank.

1. conartist (*noun*) _____

2. old fashioned (*adj*) _____

3. singer songwriter (*noun*) _____

4. chalk board (*noun*) _____

5. dirt cheap (*adj*) _____

6. pistolwhip (*verb*) _____

7. witch-hazel (*noun*) _____

8. safety razor (*noun*) _____

9. guinea-pig (*noun*) _____

10. halfmoon (*noun*) _____

11. pitch black (*adj*) _____

12. dry clean (*verb*) _____

13. chin up (*noun*) _____

14. jerry rigged (*adj*) _____

15. courtmartial (*noun*) _____

ABBREVIATIONS

For each of the following abbreviations, write out the word or words that they stand for. If one abbreviation can stand for two or more different things, write out all of them.

A. 1. f _____

2. g _____

3. m _____

4. p _____

B. 1. cm _____

2. ER _____

3. km _____

4. RR _____

C. 1. apt. _____

2. col. _____

3. doz. _____

4. gal. _____

D. 1. ABS _____

2. BBQ _____

3. DOB _____

4. HOV _____

E. 1. ETA _____

2. ICU _____

3. PIN _____

4. R & D _____

TRADEMARKS

Identify the trademarks in the following list by writing them in their proper capitalized form.

1. snooker _____
2. band-aid _____
3. dumpster _____
4. frisbee _____
5. cribbage _____
6. jet ski _____
7. kleenex _____
8. ping-pong _____
9. popsicle _____
10. rollerblade _____

IDIOMS

Fill in each blank with the letter for the idiom's definition.

1. pound of flesh ____
2. give the lie to ____
3. rub salt into someone's wounds ____
4. hang loose ____
5. keep (something) under wraps ____
6. out to lunch ____
7. cast/spread your net wide ____
8. a fish out of water ____
9. the man in the street ____
10. fall/slip through/between the cracks ____

a. a person who is in a place or situation that feels unnatural or uncomfortable

b. to make a difficult situation even worse for someone

c. to fail to be noticed or included with others

d. to show that (something) is not true

e. to remain calm and relaxed

f. the ordinary or average person

g. keep something secret

h. to try many different things so that you will have the best chance of finding something that you want

i. an amount that is owed to someone who demands to be paid

j. not aware of what is really happening

PHRASAL VERBS

Match each phrasal verb below with its definition.

1. give in ____
2. opt out ____
3. fall away ____
4. fight on ____
5. keel over ____
6. chip in ____
7. zone out ____
8. kick back ____
9. leaf out ____
10. dine in ____
11. level out ____
12. quiet down ____
13. jack in ____
14. phase out ____
15. join up ____
16. fake out ____
17. pass away ____
18. hail from ____
19. rack up ____
20. lark about ____

a. to relax and enjoy yourself
b. to stop using, making, or doing (something) gradually over a period of time
c. to die
d. to stop going up or down
e. to continue fighting
f. to become quiet or quieter
g. to stop trying to fight or resist something
h. to produce leaves
i. to choose not to do or be involved in something
j. to meet each other at a particular place
k. to behave in a silly and enjoyable way
l. to have been born or raised in (a place)
m. to become gradually less
n. to achieve or get (something) as time passes
o. to stop paying attention because you are tired, bored, etc.
p. to give something (such as money) to help a person, group, or cause
q. to deliberately deceive someone
r. to have dinner at home
s. to stop doing something
t. to fall down suddenly

UNDEFINED WORDS

For each of the following undefined words, an incomplete definition has been provided. In each blank, complete the definition by writing the headword of the entry where the word can be found.

1. **alertly** *adv* : in an _____ manner

2. **geographic** *adj* : of or relating to _____

3. **rancorous** *adj* : filled with _____

4. **reactionary** *adj* : resembling a _____

5. **bleakness** *noun* : the quality or state of being _____

6. **mayoral** *adj* : of or relating to a _____

7. **embargo** *verb* : to place an _____ on something

8. **twentieth** *adj* : being the number _____ in order

9. **archaeologist** *noun* : a person who studies _____

10. **rapacity** *noun* : the quality or state of being _____

11. **tasseled** *adj* : having a _____

12. **thuggish** *adj* : resembling a _____

13. **sabbatical** *adj* : of or relating to a _____

14. **shortsightedness** *noun* : the quality or state of being _____

15. **languorous** *adj* : in a state of _____

PRONUNCIATIONS

A. In each list below, circle the words that have the same pronunciation.

1. rein
   reign
   range
   rang
   rain

2. peak
   peek
   pike
   pick
   pique

B. Identify the words that have the following pronunciations.

1. /ˈdʒækət/ _____
2. /ˈpædl̩/ _____
3. /ˈfɪkʃən/ _____
4. /ˈhaɪˌweɪ/ _____
5. /ˈmɛθəd/ _____

C. What consonants in the following words are not pronounced?

1. heir _____
2. corps _____
3. receipt _____
4. soften _____
5. yacht _____

VARIANT SPELLINGS

What is the more common spelling of each of these words?

1. ameba _____
2. bosun _____
3. caldron _____
4. djinn _____
5. filo _____
6. jibe _____
7. kaftan _____
8. medivac _____
9. nosey _____
10. pricy _____
11. manikin _____
12. olde _____
13. man-size _____
14. rhumba _____
15. rock 'n' roll _____

DEFINITIONS: SENSES

Look up *sense 2* of each headword in the first column below (be sure to look at the correct homograph), and write the letter of its basic meaning in the blank.

1. ¹**ace** _____   a. autumn
2. ¹**boat** _____   b. not sinful
3. ¹**boot** _____   c. symbol
4. ¹**bug** _____   d. container
5. **chaste** _____   e. illness
6. ²**fall** _____   f. haven
7. ¹**flip-flop** _____   g. skilled person
8. ¹**thirst** _____   h. kick
9. ¹**harbor** _____   i. flat surface
10. **jacket** _____   j. game
11. ¹**token** _____   k. shell
12. **olive** _____   l. personality
13. **nature** _____   m. offensive word
14. **oath** _____   n. color
15. ¹**pitch** _____   o. change of opinion
16. ¹**plane** _____   p. respect
17. ¹**shuck** _____   q. record
18. **treasure hunt** _____   r. covering
19. **obeisance** _____   s. desire
20. ¹**tab** _____   t. baseball throw

DEFINITIONS: SUBSENSES

Look up each boldface word below (be sure to look at the headword that has the same homograph number attached to it), and write the number and letter of the subsense (e.g., "2c") that is being used in the phrase shown.

1. set a ¹**date** _____

2. trip and ¹**fall** _____

3. hired ¹**hands** _____

4. ¹**keep** kosher _____

5. a ¹**labor** dispute _____

6. a ¹**late** riser _____

7. a publicity ¹**machine** _____

8. ²**narrow** the search _____

9. on every **odd**-numbered page _____

10. divorce ¹**papers** _____

TYPES OF DEFINITIONS

For each of the phrases or senses below, fill in the blank with the symbol at the beginning of the definition: ":," "—," or "◇."
(A number following a word, as in "**naturally 4**," is the sense number.)

1. ¹**short 8** _____

2. **answer to a name** _____

3. **got game** _____

4. **naturally 4** _____

5. **gratis** _____

6. **of all things** _____

7. **take turns** _____

8. **one jump ahead** _____

9. **unaccounted for** _____

10. **in back of** _____

SYNONYMS AND ANTONYMS

A. Write a synonym for each of these nouns.

1. bed-and-breakfast _____

2. beeper _____

3. downspout _____

4. femur _____

5. garbanzo _____

6. pinkie _____

7. belly button _____

8. sad sack _____

9. vacuity _____

10. thong _____

B. What is the antonym given at each of these entries?

1. **victory** _____

2. **²standard** _____

3. **legalize** _____

4. **¹make 19a** _____

5. **supple** _____

EXAMPLE SENTENCES AND PHRASES

A. Fill in each blank with the *first* example sentence for each of the following entries.

1. **mythology** _____

2. **²rib** _____

3. **babysit** _____

4. **jeans** _____

5. **rusty** _____

B. For each of the following words, read the *first* example for each specified sense (for example, the first example at sense 4a of ¹break), and answer the question about it.

1. **¹break 4a** What is the direct object of "broke"? _____

2. **¹calm 1** What pronoun does "calm" modify? _____

3. **¹except** What is the object of "except"? _____

4. **¹whistle 1a** What verb has "whistle" as its direct object? _____

5. **squabble** What is the sentence's subject? _____

6. **¹honeymoon 1** What preposition does "honeymoon" follow? _____

7. **milieu** What two adjectives modify "milieu"? _____ _____

8. **²report 1** What noun is the direct object of "reported"? _____

9. **apprehend 1** What is the subject of "apprehended"? _____

10. **diction 1** What adjective modifies "diction"? _____

11. **¹wipe 3** What is the direct object of "wiped"? _____

12. **²cover 1** What verb has "cover" as its direct object? _____

13. ³**plenty** What adjective is modified by "plenty"? _____

14. ²**beyond 2** What noun is the object of "beyond"? _____

15. ¹**multiple 1** What noun is modified by "multiple"?

_____

16. **pollute** What word is the subject of "polluted"? _____

17. **offend 1** What word is the subject of "offended"? _____

18. **intensify 1** What word is the subject of "intensify"?

_____

19. **itself** What noun does "itself" refer to? _____

20. **spectator** What verb has "spectators" as its subject?

_____

21. **frigid 1** What noun is modified by "frigid"? _____

22. **delicate 1b** What noun is modified by "delicate"? _____

23. **enhance** What is the direct object of "enhance"? _____

24. ¹**whisper 2** What is the object of the preposition following "whispered"? _____

25. ²**license 1** What noun is the direct object of "licensed"?

_____

26. ¹**halt 1** What noun is the direct object of "halted"?

_____

27. ¹**apart 1** What verb is modified by "apart"? _____

28. ²**pivot** What two verbs have the subject "dancers"?

_____ _____

29. **modify 1** What are the sentence's other three verbs?

_____ _____ _____

30. **vitamin 1** What is the sentence's other direct object?

_____

BOLDFACE PHRASES IN EXAMPLES

A. Write the explanation that is given in square brackets for each of the following phrases.

    1. *took a jab at* _____

    2. *hit the slopes* _____

    3. *taking the trouble* _____

    4. *on the face of the earth* _____

    5. *get the idea* _____

    6. *paid obeisance* _____

    7. *stark raving mad* _____

    8. *hate mail* _____

    9. *close/seal the deal* _____

    10. *a brief word* _____

B. Look up each of the expressions in boldface italic type below. (Each will appear at the entry for one or more of its important words.) Then cross out the word or phrase and write an equivalent expression above it.

    1. Stock prices haven't yet *hit rock bottom*.

    2. You need to *keep your voice down* while in the library.

    3. By November he couldn't pay his bills and was in a terrible *fix*.

    4. I *can't stand* the smell of cigarette smoke.

    5. It may be the greatest threat facing *modern man*.

    6. The TV host was talking *a mile a minute*.

    7. Their daughter's teacher spoke about her *in glowing terms*.

    8. "*Grab a seat*," he said. "I'll bring some beer."

    9. He turned up the *sound* on the television.

    10. Organizing these files is *no picnic*.

"— + ADVERB/PREPOSITION" NOTES

A. Look up the entry for each word in italics below, and fill in each blank with the proper adverb or preposition.

1. His *defiance* ____ the law started when he was only 15.

2. He wanted to *neaten* ____ the living room before she arrived.

3. They spent too much time *tending* ____ their business and not enough time relaxing.

4. He could only understand a *bit* ____ the lecture.

5. The new computer program was highly *prone* ____ errors.

6. On Monday you will be *tested* ____ all the past tenses.

7. All the soil was *tested* ____ pollution from the nearby chemical plant.

8. No one noticed that the men at the next table had been *eavesdropping* ____ their conversation.

9. His aunt had a *mania* ____ British TV comedies.

10. She gave her sister *props* ____ staying cool when testifying in court against her husband.

B. Where necessary, cross out the incorrect adverb or preposition after the word in italics and write the correct adverb or preposition above it.

1. The new factory was a *blight* in the landscape.

2. The area where the accident occurred had been *blocked* off.

3. He again *proposed* at his girlfriend, and again she rejected him.

4. They *edged* for the other team in the final minutes of the game.

5. The branches had to be *pruned* out every few years.

PLURAL FORMS OF NOUNS

What is the plural form of these nouns?

1. attorney at law _____
2. child _____
3. criterion _____
4. foot _____
5. hero _____

6. moose _____
7. mouse _____
8. silo _____
9. wife _____
10. analysis _____

FORMS AND TENSES OF VERBS

Write out in full the *past, past participle,* and *present participle* forms of the following verbs.

1. fall _____
2. decide _____
3. forgive _____
4. shed _____
5. swim _____

COMPARATIVE AND SUPERLATIVE FORMS

Write the comparative and superlative forms for each of the following adjectives.

1. neat _____
2. brave _____
3. fast _____
4. radiant _____
5. heavy _____
6. representative _____
7. jaded _____

8. raw _____

9. just _____

10. heavily _____

11. free _____

12. fun _____

13. good _____

14. idealistic _____

15. hollow _____

"COUNT," "NONCOUNT," "SINGULAR," AND "PLURAL" NOUNS

A. Circle the noncount nouns below.

1. buffalo	6. mail
2. diction	7. nectar
3. gap	8. optics
4. jellyfish	9. packaging
5. laity	10. spaghetti

**B. Which numbered senses or subsenses of these nouns (e.g., "3," "2c")
are always treated as plural?**

1. directions _____

2. economics _____

3. faculty _____

4. police _____

5. proceeds _____

**C. After each of these nouns, write whether they are labeled as *singular*
or *usually singular*.**

1. din _____

2. glut _____

3. knack _____

4. minimum_____

5. onset _____

TRANSITIVE AND INTRANSITIVE VERBS

A. For each of the following verbs, look up the verb's first *transitive* sense or subsense, and write the direct object for the first verbal illustration that appears there. For example, for the verb **emanate**, the example is "Some radioactive substances can *emanate* [=(more commonly) *emit*] radiation for many years," so you would write "radiation" as the direct object.

1. earn _____

2. fear _____

3. heal _____

4. infect _____

5. join _____

B. Circle any of the following verbs that are *always intransitive.*

1. facilitate
2. laugh
3. march
4. occur
5. pause
6. faint
7. limp
8. exist
9. gallop
10. grade

C. For each verb in italics below, identify the sense or subsense (e.g., "2," "4a") that the sentence illustrates. If the verb is transitive, circle its direct object.

1. The company has *advertised* for an accountant. _____

2. They *chose* my roommate as the team captain. _____

3. Some ducks were *feeding* in his neighbor's pond. _____

4. She *questioned* his ability to complete the work. _____

5. The fuel shortage is *reaching* a critical point. _____

REGIONAL LABELS: AMERICAN AND BRITISH USAGE

A. Each of the following terms has a meaning that is specifically American. For that meaning, what is the British equivalent?

1. out-box _____

2. corn _____

3. advice column _____

4. garbage truck _____

5. thumbtack _____

6. insurance adjuster _____

7. instant replay _____

8. kerosene _____

9. mailbox _____

10. oatmeal _____

B. Each of the following terms has a meaning that is specifically British. For that meaning, what is the American equivalent?

1. bonnet _____

2. saloon _____

3. diversion _____

4. full stop _____

5. identity parade _____

6. nappy _____

7. patience _____

8. rucksack _____

9. spanner _____

10. visiting card _____

SUBJECT, STATUS, AND REGISTER LABELS

A. For each entry in the first column, write the letter of the correct subject label in the blank. A number following a word (as in "**dominant 3**") is the number of the individual sense that has the label.

1. **clause** ____   a. *grammar*

2. **dominant 3** ____   b. *music*

3. **Hail Mary 2** ____   c. *psychology*

4. **legato** ____   d. *American football*

5. **projection 6** ____   e. *biology*

B. For each entry in the first column, write the letter of the correct status or register label in the blank next to it. If there are two labels, include both.

1. **amatory** ____   a. *informal*

2. **belle** ____   b. *formal*

3. **face time** ____   c. *literary*

4. **garner** ____   d. *old-fashioned*

5. **purloin** ____   e. *humorous*

6. **crappy** ____   f. *disapproving*

7. **damn** ____   g. *slang*

8. **diddly** ____   h. *impolite*

9. **freaking** ____   i. *offensive*

10. **primo** ____

"ESPECIALLY," "SPECIFICALLY," "BROADLY," AND "ALSO" LABELS

Write the definition that is introduced by each label below.

1. **AWOL**, *broadly* _____

2. **beast**, *especially* _____

3. **¹dish 1a**, *specifically* _____

4. **olive drab**, *also* _____

5. **Easterner**, *especially* _____

6. **¹gig**, *broadly* _____

7. **²negative**, *also* _____

8. **bacillus**, *also* _____

9. **bunny**, *especially* _____

10. **radish**, *also* _____

11. **¹game 2b**, *specifically* _____

12. **textile**, *especially* _____

13. **hardware 2**, *especially* _____

14. **Native American**, *especially* _____

15. **calumny**, *also* _____

"ALWAYS USED . . . ,"
"NOT USED . . . ," ETC. LABELS

Look up each entry below (if necessary) and read its italicized label ("*always used*...," "*not used*...," etc.), then circle the number of each grammatically correct sentence.

1. ¹**absent**   He had a loving mother but an absent father.

2. ²**adult**   She worked in the field of adult literacy.

3. **deserving**   The dinner and entertainment were deserving praise.

4. **glad**   A glad clerk answered all their questions.

5. **hungry**   After several failures, they were hungry for success.

6. **apiece**   The tickets cost apiece ten dollars.

7. **galore**   There was candy galore, and the children grabbed for it greedily.

8. ³**elect**   The elect president was choosing his advisers.

9. ²**enough**   Even though they're rich, they never feel rich enough.

10. **aplenty**   There were aplenty peaches hanging from the tree.

11. **glide**   Three skiers were gliding the slope.

12. ¹**knock**   The wind knocked on him backwards.

13. ¹**march**   The army had marched north again.

14. **modern-day**   He's a saint who is modern-day.

15. ²**parade**   The protesters paraded City Hall shouting slogans.

FIGURATIVE USE

A. What example phrase does the dictionary give for the figurative use of each of the following words?

1. allergic _____

2. bejeweled _____

3. gatekeeper _____

4. key _____

5. nourishing _____

B. Using the words *behind, navigable, big leagues, obituary*, and *prologue*, complete the following sentences.

1. The beginning of his political campaign ended up being a
   _____ to disaster.

2. She was always an excellent accountant, but she didn't really join the
   _____ until she moved to New York City.

3. They've left their unhappy past _____ and are excited
   about the future.

4. They have an easily _____ Web site; it only takes a few
   seconds to find anything.

5. He lost a lot of money last year, but it's too soon to write his
   _____.

"SEE" AND "SEE ALSO" CROSS-REFERENCES

At the following entries, what entries are you told to "see" or "see also"?

1. **baseman** _____
2. **magnesia** _____
3. **basket** _____
4. **hat** _____
5. **owner** _____
6. **gap** _____
7. **grape** _____
8. **jewelry** _____
9. **¹jockey** _____
10. **keg** _____

"COMPARE" CROSS-REFERENCES

What words are you invited to "compare" at these entries?

1. **paternal** _____
2. **queen-size** _____
3. **¹peaked** _____
4. **radius** _____
5. **patriotism** _____
6. **ego** _____
7. **¹earmark** _____
8. **³paddle** _____
9. **half-moon** _____
10. **dashboard** _____

SYNONYM PARAGRAPHS

Look up each word in italics below, then cross it out and replace it with a synonym that is more appropriate for the sentence.

1. The dead squirrel's body was *decaying* on the side of the road.

2. A lack of sleep can *injure* your memory.

3. You can't change the *laws* in the middle of the game.

4. Denise *prizes* her nephews and the time she spends with them.

5. A popular governor has the *dominion* to change public opinion.

6. The museum had large collections from *antique* Greece.

7. The *charge* of the shoes had been marked down from $95 to $70.

8. He had always had an *alarm* of high places.

9. The pool table is kept in a *moist* and musty basement.

10. The spray contains a chemical that is *deadly* to insects.

PHRASES DISCUSSED IN ✧ NOTES

Look up each phrase and read the sentence following the ✧, then circle the letter of the sentence below that comes closest to the original sentence's meaning.

1. The comedian had the audience *rolling in the aisles*.

    a. The audience was so angry that they left the show.

    b. The audience was laughing very hard.

    c. The audience wasn't paying attention to the comedian.

2. The latest *flavor of the month* is a 19-year-old jazz singer from Kansas City.

    a. The 19-year-old jazz singer has been popular for a long time.

    b. The 19-year-old jazz singer is popular with a small number of people.

    c. The 19-year-old jazz singer has just become popular but probably won't remain so.

3. The company's *death knell* was the departure of its main investor.

    a. The departure of the company's main investor caused it to fail.

    b. The departure of the company's main investor caused it to be more successful.

    c. The company's main investor died soon after departing.

4. The opinions in her newspaper column always *go against the grain*.

    a. The opinions in her newspaper column aren't shared by many people.

    b. The opinions in her newspaper column are always insulting and offensive.

    c. The opinions in her newspaper column change frequently.

5. The rumors were *blown out of proportion* by the news media.

    a. The rumors were not reported by the news media.

    b. The news media exploded the rumors.

    c. The news media made the rumors sound more important than they were.

6. Her opponent seemed to *have no chinks in his armor*.

    a. Her opponent seemed to have no flaws or weaknesses.

    b. Her opponent was easy to defeat.

    c. Her opponent refused to surrender.

7. He was working *on autopilot* when he made the mistake.

    a. He was traveling on an airplane when he made the mistake.

    b. He was working while drunk when he made the mistake.

    c. He was doing work without thinking about it when he made the mistake.

8. The car is *in a class by itself*.

    a. Only one car of that model was manufactured.

    b. The car is of a high quality that no other car matches.

    c. The car is parked in a garage with no other cars.

9. His golf clubs are *collecting dust* in the closet.

    a. His golf clubs are broken.

    b. His golf clubs aren't being used.

    c. His golf clubs are cleaning the closet.

10. The best police officers have *ice water in their veins*.

    a. The best police officers are tough and brave.

    b. The best police officers are very cold.

    c. The best police officers drink a lot of liquids.

USAGE PARAGRAPHS

Answer the following questions, using the information given in a usage paragraph.

1. In British English, what pronoun (*this* or *that*) do you use when asking who you are speaking to on the phone? _____

2. What phrases can be used instead of the incorrect phrase "be let"?

   _____

3. What type of noun is *amount* usually used with? _____

4. In informal speech and writing, when is *neither* sometimes used with a plural verb? _____

5. Which preposition is used after *different* in British English but not in U.S. English? _____

6. In U.S. English, what type of verb is *family* used with?

   _____

7. What are the usual negative forms of "have got"?

   _____

8. Which of these questions is usually asked in a friendly way: "What's the matter?" or "What's the matter with you?"

9. Which of these three terms is the least likely to be considered offensive: *American Indian*, *Indian*, or *Native American*?

10. When *bring* and *take* have opposite meanings, *bring* suggests that something is moving in what direction? _____

ILLUSTRATIONS

A. Look at the illustration for geometry. What basic geometric shape is represented by each of the following objects?

1. tree trunk _____

2. planet _____

3. box _____

4. book page _____

5. chessboard _____

B. Compare the sizes of the objects and animals at these entries.

1. Look at the illustration for **ball,** and number the following balls by size from smallest to largest (1, 2, 3, 4, 5).

   basketball ____
   volleyball ____
   cricket ball ____
   golf ball ____
   softball ____

2. Look at the illustration for **rodent**, and number the following rodents from smallest to largest.

   mouse ____
   woodchuck ____
   porcupine ____
   squirrel ____
   beaver ____

3. Look at the illustration for **stringed instrument**, and number the following instruments from smallest to largest.

   cello ____
   double bass ____
   viola ____
   violin ____
   harp ____

C. Look at the color illustrations for clothing, and answer the following questions.

1. Circle any of the following that are undergarments: camisole, half slip, halter, tank top, briefs, cardigan

2. Circle any of the following that cover the legs: sarong, pantyhose, leotard, pajamas, tights

3. Circle any of the following that are most commonly worn by men: vest, sari, sport coat, suspenders, muumuu

GEOGRAPHICAL NAMES

Use the list of geographical names, which begins on p. 1910 of the dictionary, to answer the following questions.

1. What do you call a person from the Philippines? _____

2. Where is Ben Nevis? _____

3. What is Cozumel? _____

4. What is another name for Ivory Coast? _____

5. What two countries border on the Jordan River?

   _____   _____

6. What is Mauna Loa? _____

7. Where is Patagonia? _____

8. Where did the Silk Road begin and end? _____

9. Does the Caspian Sea have freshwater or salt water? _____

10. What is the former name of Yangon? _____

11. Where was ancient Carthage? _____

12. What two seas are connected by the Bosporus?

    _____   _____

13. What country do the Canary Islands belong to?

    _____

14. Is Palau a possession or an independent country? _____

15. What is the modern name of Byzantium? _____

16. What two countries share the island of Timor?

_____ _____

17. What two ancient countries had a city named Thebes?

_____ _____

18. What country does Tahiti belong to? _____

19. Where is Mt. Kilimanjaro? _____

20. What two countries share the Riviera?

_____ _____

GRAMMAR

A. What is the part of speech for the word in italics in each of the sentences below? Use the following list of terms to fill in the blanks.

gerund   linking verb

indefinite pronoun   modal verb

demonstrative pronoun   interrogative adverb

demonstrative adjective   coordinating conjunction

predicate adjective   adverb

1. Everything *seems* to be in order. _____

2. *Smoking* is not allowed in the theater. _____

3. Those shoes are nice, but I like *these* better.

_____

4. Would you mind if I came *along*? _____

5. If you tell me your secret, I promise not to tell *anyone*.

_____

6. *These* twelve-hour work days have been very difficult on us.

_____

7. She said that she *can't* come to the party.

_____

8. *Where* are you from? _____

9. My son *and* I went to the store. _____

10. The test was really *difficult*. _____

B. In the following sentences, cross out any grammatical errors and write the correct version above them.

1. We don't have many milk, but there are any doughnuts.

2. She didn't went home after the movie, and she still haven't called.

3. They were enjoyed seeing the California, but they didn't enjoyed American food.

4. When he is young, he was read about dinosaurs all the time.

5. He is taken the car somewhere; I don't knowing when he will be back.

6. The pasta would be better if it has more salt.

7. Sun shined brightly in morning, but sky became cloudy in afternoon.

8. You aren't going to work today, is it?

9. She showed me her sports BMW green beautiful car.

10. He is loving to go to nightclubs, but I am always preferring to stay in home.

C. Rewrite the following sentences. Change any active voice to passive, and change any passive voice to active.

1. The test is being taken by Alex today, and the same one will be taken by his brother next spring. _____

_____

_____

2. We'll show some short films first, and then the awards will be given by the CEO. _____

_____

_____

3. The dinner had been prepared by his parents, and his sister brought dessert. _____

_____

_____

4. Big department stores are preferred by many people, but others prefer smaller shops. _____

_____

5. The Japanese team was beaten by the Australians, but Spain defeated the United States. _____

_____

CONTRACTIONS

A. In the following sentences, cross out any words that can be contracted and write the contraction above them.

1. If you had told me you were coming, I would have cooked something.

2. They are on their way to the party, so we will meet them there.

3. Even if we had not turned onto that road, we would still be lost.

4. It does not matter which day it happened—I could not have come.

5. Jeff said he would be at the theater when we arrived, but he was not.

B. In the following sentences, cross out the contractions and write the complete words above them.

1. I wasn't going to ask about your hair, but you've made me curious.

2. You wouldn't even know what a mongoose was if I hadn't told you.

3. The package hasn't arrived yet and isn't expected to arrive until tomorrow.

4. I should've known that her brother wasn't coming until Thursday.

5. You shouldn't reply unless you're certain that you want the job.

6. I dunno if Mom'll let me.

7. He's gotta give 'em an answer by tomorrow.

8. Lemme know if you're gonna be there.

9. There's a better one that's sorta green with white dots.

10. We'd kinda like to keep our jobs.

PREFIXES AND SUFFIXES

A. Draw a line from each prefix in the first column to a word from the second column to make another word that appears in the dictionary.

1.	anti-	judge
2.	co-	alcoholic
3.	dis-	frost
4.	in-	bacterial
5.	inter-	agreeable
6.	mis-	conscious
7.	non-	national
8.	de-	constitutional
9.	sub-	consistent
10.	un-	author

B. Draw a line from each word in the first column to a suffix in the second column to make another word that appears in the dictionary.

1.	up	-al
2.	good	-ation
3.	peace	-ative
4.	talk	-ful
5.	person	-ism
6.	slow	-less
7.	poison	-ly
8.	child	-ness
9.	Marx	-ous
10.	flirt	-ward

C. Using the list on p. 1958, add a prefix to each word in the first column to form a word that matches the following definition.

1.	_____pay	: to pay for (something) before you receive or use it
2.	_____standard	: below what is considered standard, normal, or acceptable
3.	_____fill	: to fill a container with too much of something
4.	_____natal	: relating to the period of time following the birth of a child

5. _____lateral   : involving only one group or country

6. _____violent   : not using or involving violence

7. _____continental   : going across a continent

8. _____state   : to state or report something incorrectly

9. _____productive   : not helpful

10. _____planetary   : existing or occurring between planets

ENGLISH WORD ROOTS

For each of the following words, write the root you find in it, and then write the root's meaning in parentheses. For example, for _illuminate_ you would write "lum (light)." If you find two roots in a single word, list them both.

1. armada _____

2. audible _____

3. biography _____

4. dictionary _____

5. fidelity _____

6. metric _____

7. potential _____

8. renovate _____

9. telescope _____

10. unsanitary _____

SPELLING RULES

A. Underline each of the following words that is spelled correctly. For each misspelled word, write out the correct spelling.

    1. accomodate _____

    2. catagory _____

    3. embarrass _____

    4. innoculate _____

    5. occured _____

B. What is the usual American spelling of the following words?

    1. meagre _____

    2. oestrogen _____

    3. realise _____

    4. travelled _____

    5. fervour _____

C. For each adjective in the list below, write the comparative form (ending in -*er*). For each verb, write the present-tense third-person form (ending in -*s*). For each noun, write the plural form.

    1. sash _____   9. basis _____

    2. crazy _____   10. donkey _____

    3. confess _____   11. see _____

    4. thief _____   12. lorry _____

    5. glad _____   13. brunch _____

    6. sew _____   14. savvy _____

    7. sharp _____   15. fade _____

    8. CEO _____

THE SPELLING OF DIFFERENT SOUNDS IN ENGLISH

1. In the lists on pp. 1968-69, find the three words that show how "o" is pronounced in the words *bomb*, *catacomb*, and *tomb*.

   _____

2. Find all the words in the lists in which "ou" is pronounced in different ways.

   _____

3. Which of the seven spellings of the /k/ sound never appear at the beginning of a word? (You may need to look in the main part of the dictionary.)

   _____

STYLE: PUNCTUATION

Insert the missing hyphens, commas, colons, quotation marks, and apostrophes in the following paragraphs.

On April 18 19 2009 Rexs Tavern will host its second ever charity darts tournament to benefit the Tall Oaks Boys and Girls Camp of Manchester.

Last year there were twenty five competitors and Jerome White the owner of Rexs says he is hoping to bring in double that number this year. The top prizes for this years event will be a state of the art GPS system and an MP3 player. These prizes will be donated by Rick Davidson of Ricks Electronics. Hats mugs and gift certificates will also be offered as door prizes.

Its going to be a great time said White. Well have all of our best beers on tap and an array of live performers and its all going to a great cause.

The winner of last years tournament Michael Jones said that he is prepared to defend his title. Holding a rabbits foot for good luck Jones said It was a blast last year. I met a lot of good friends and hopefully therell be more people competing this year.

In addition to the entry fees White said two thirds of all food and beverage sales from the tournament will be donated to Tall Oaks. Two other local businesses will help to sponsor the event Hendersons Import Auto Sales and Martinellis Pizza.

The entry fee is twenty dollars. White said that players will not need to pre register for the tournament but those who wish to enter should arrive to the tavern no later than two oclock on April 18.

STYLE: CAPITALS AND ITALICS

In the paragraphs below, circle any letter that should be capitalized, and underline any word or phrase that should appear in italics.

andersons book shop in west charlestown will host a signing and lecture by financial expert suzanne walker, author of the best-selling investment guide going for broke: speculation in a pool of risk, on saturday at 2:00 p.m.

walkers first book, take the money and run, was chosen by the new york times as one of the notable books of 2003, and was a finalist for awards from the magazines fortune and business week. going for broke has already sold 200,000 copies.

publisher's weekly called going for broke "a must-read for anyone who's looking to invest in the market." cara richardson of the wall street journal wrote, "in this era of specialized investing and overspeculation, it's become more difficult for the amateur investor to make rational decisions about where to put his or her money. going for broke answers those questions in plain english that's a pleasure to read."

if you would like to reserve a seat for this event, please call lori mcnulty at (242) 555-2727.

COMMON FIRST NAMES

List five names (either formal names or nicknames) that are used by *both* men and women.

1. _____
2. _____
3. _____
4. _____
5. _____

MONEY

Circle the letter of the correct answer for each question.

1. Which type of currency exists but is rarely used?
   a. Canadian $1 coin   b. U.S. 50¢ coin   c. U.K. £20 note

2. What type of currency is called the "loonie"?
   a. British pound   b. U.S. $1 coin   c. Canadian $1 coin

3. Which type of card allows a store to take cash from your account immediately?
   a. credit card   b. debit card   c. ATM card

4. Which of the following U.S. coins is the least valuable?
   a. dime   b. nickel   c. quarter

5. Which of the following normally requires the highest fees?
   a. cash advance   b. ATM cash withdrawal   c. use of debit card

NUMBERS

Write the following numbers as indicated.

1. Spell out 1,000,000. _____

2. Write "one hundred thousand" in digits. _____

3. Write the Roman numeral for 2009. _____

4. Spell out 95th. _____

5. Spell out 1,500 in two different ways.

   _____   _____

6. Spell out 5/8. _____

7. Spell out 2½. _____

8. Write .15 as it would be spoken. _____

9. Write 0.654 as it would be spoken. _____

10. Write the number MDCCCXII in the ordinary way. _____

WEIGHTS AND MEASURES

Circle the larger of each pair of quantities below.

1. metric ton / ton
2. liter / quart
3. acre / hectare
4. meter / yard
5. pound / kilogram

DATES

The 4th day of March in the year 2005 can be written in several different forms. Write it in five different ways, as indicated.

1. (American style, using numbers and letters) _____

2. (British style, numbers and letters) _____

3. (American style, numbers only) _____

4. (British style, numbers only) _____

5. (ISO style) _____

HOLIDAYS

Circle the letter of the correct answer for each question.

1. In which country is Columbus Day a government holiday?

   a. United States   b. United Kingdom   c. Canada   d. Australia

2. Which country does not observe Boxing Day?

   a. United Kingdom   b. Canada   c. United States   d. Australia

3. Which country celebrates Victoria Day?

   a. Australia   b. Canada   c. United Kingdom   d. United States

4. Which countries observe Labor Day as a government holiday?

   a. Canada   b. Australia   c. United States   d. United Kingdom

5. When is Remembrance Day observed?

   a. Feb. 14   b. July 4   c. Oct. 31   d. Nov. 11

ENVELOPE ADDRESSES

Identify the error in each of the following addresses.

1. Dr. and Mrs. David R. Pacheco
   6305 Sunset Gardens, SW
   NM 87121
   U.S.A.

   _____

2. Miss Jean MacRobbie
   Career Development Centre
   University of Stirling
   STIRLING   FK9 4LA
   Scotland

   _____

3. Mr. Robert L. Simmons
   573 Cloutier Dr.
   Winnipeg, MB 333 868
   Canada

   _____

4. Judy Prendergast, M.D.
   Royal Brisbane & Women's Hospital
   Butterfield St. & Bowen Bridge Rd.
   HERSTON 4029
   Australia

   _____

5. Ms. Charlotte Liu
   31 Huntington Street
   New Salem, AL 0630
   U.S.A.

   _____

E-MAIL, LETTERS, RÉSUMÉS, AND MEMOS

1. Write three formal closings for a letter.

   _____

   _____

   _____

2. List at least three facts that should *not* be stated in a résumé.

   _____

   _____

   _____

3. List three elements that are included in a business letter but *not* in a memo.

   _____

   _____

   _____

Alphabetical Order

Words are entered in this dictionary in standard alphabetical order. The order is not affected by spaces between words, by hyphens or other punctuation, or by capital letters. Phrasal verbs always appear at the entry for their first word. Undefined words are entered at the end of the entries for words from which they are derived. When a symbol or number is part of a word (as in R&B), the word is alphabetized as if the symbol or number were written out using letters. Here are three sequences of dictionary entries:

AOB	alloy	arms race
A-OK	all-powerful	arm-twisting
A1	all-purpose	arm wrestling
aorta	all right	army

Guidewords

At the top of every page in the dictionary are two words, called *guidewords*, which indicate the first and last main entry words on that page.

Most Common Words

This dictionary highlights 3,000 basic English words that Merriam-Webster editors selected as being the most important for learners to know. These common English words are underlined in blue at their entries.

Homographs

An entry word, or *headword,* may appear more than once in the dictionary, with a different small number attached to it each time (for example, ¹**act**, ²**act**). Each numbered headword, called a *homograph*, usually represents a different part of speech (noun, verb, etc.). However, sometimes two homographs represent the *same* part of speech but are not related to each other at all and have two very different meanings. For example, since there are two different verbs spelled *lie* and two different nouns spelled *lie*, you will see the four homographs ¹**lie** (verb), ²**lie** (noun), ³**lie** (verb), and ⁴**lie** (noun).

Additional highlighted examples of homographs are shown on p. 10a of the dictionary.

Compounds

A compound is a term formed by combining two or more words. Some compounds are closed up, with no space between the words (for example, *birthplace*). However, many compounds consist of two or more separate words (e.g., *high heels*), and many have hyphens between the words (e.g., *no-show*). All compounds in this dictionary have their own individual entries (except for phrasal verbs, which are always shown at the entry for their first word).

For additional information about the way that compounds are formed, see p. 1973 of the dictionary.

Abbreviations

Many abbreviations have their own entries in the dictionary. For a discussion of the punctuation and capitalization of abbreviations, see p. 1975 of the dictionary.

Trademarks

Trademarks are the names of companies or their commercial products. They are always capitalized. Many well-known trademarks are entered in the dictionary.

Idioms

Thousands of idioms are defined in this dictionary. Most are defined at the entry for an important word in the phrase; for example, *make no bones about* is entered after the main senses at **¹bone**. If there is more than one important word, as in *cut the mustard*, the idiom is defined at the entry for one of the words, while the entry for the other important word includes a note that directs you to the entry where the phrase is defined. In this case, the phrase is defined at **mustard**, and a note, "*cut the mustard* see MUSTARD," appears at **¹cut**.

Phrasal Verbs

A phrasal verb consists of an ordinary verb and an adverb, a preposition, or both, and has a meaning different from the meaning of the ordinary verb. Each phrasal verb in this dictionary is defined at the entry for its main verb; for example, *move on* is entered after the main senses at **¹move**.

Phrasal verbs are discussed at length on pp. 1943-44 of the dictionary.

Undefined Words

Boldface words without definitions appear at the end of some dictionary entries. The meaning of these words can be understood when you know the meaning of the main entry word that they are related to. Many of these words end in a suffix like *-ly* or *-ness*, and you can understand the word's meaning by combining the meaning of the base word (the main entry word) and the meaning of the suffix. For example, the adverb **judicially**, which appears without a definition at the end of the entry for the adjective **judicial**, can be defined as "in a judicial way."

Pronunciations

The dictionary's pronunciations are provided in the International Phonetic Alphabet (IPA). Its symbols are explained in the lists on pp. 22a and 1994 of the

dictionary. Pronunciations are shown between a pair of slashes / / following the entry word. Only the most common pronunciations for a particular word are shown, and pronunciations are not shown at every entry. The Pronunciations section of Using the Dictionary on pp. 11a-12a discusses how and when pronunciations are shown at dictionary entries.

Variant Spellings

Some English words can be spelled in more than one way. When an entry in this dictionary shows two spellings separated by *or* (for example, "**facade** *or* **façade**"), both spellings are common. If two spellings are separated by *also* (for example, "**guerrilla** *also* **guerilla**"), the second spelling is much less common. Whenever two spellings would not appear near each other alphabetically in the dictionary, each is given its own entry; the entry for the less common spelling directs you to the entry for the more common spelling (for example, "**bannister** *variant spelling of* BANISTER").

For a discussion and examples of how U.S. and British variant spellings are shown in the dictionary, see the Spelling section of Using the Dictionary on pp. 12a-13a of the dictionary. See also p. 1967.

Definitions: Senses

Many words in this dictionary have more than one meaning, or *sense*. When there is more than one sense, each separate sense begins with a boldface number: **1, 2**, etc. The most common sense is generally listed first.

Definitions: Subsenses

A numbered sense may be divided into *subsenses* when two or more uses of a word are very closely related, or when one sense of a word has two specific uses. Each subsense begins with a letter: **a**, **b**, etc.

Types of Definitions

Most definitions in this dictionary begin with a boldface colon (:), but other definitions begin with a dash (—), and others begin with the symbol ✧. The definitions that begin with — describe how a word or phrase is used; those that begin with ✧ are written as complete sentences.

Synonyms and Antonyms

Synonyms are words that have the same meaning. Many entries in this dictionary include a synonym written in SMALL CAPITAL LETTERS at the end of their definitions. For some entries, the only definition shown is a synonym; for example, sense 2 of **exam** is defined by "EXAMINATION 1b"). The note "called also" at the end of an entry is also used to indicate a synonym; for example, **garbage truck** has this note at the end of its entry: "— called also (*Brit*) *dustcart*." Other synonyms are shown in square brackets within example sentences and phrases; for example, **rambunctious** has this example: "a class full of *rambunctious* [=*boisterous*, (*Brit*) *rumbustious*] children."

Antonyms are words that have opposite meanings. In this dictionary, when a word has an antonym, it is shown at the end of the entry or sense. Antonyms are introduced with the word "opposite" and written in small capital letters.

Example Sentences and Phrases

Most entries in the dictionary include at least one sentence or phrase that gives an example of how the word is used. The examples appear in blue type, separated from each other by small blue squares. Some examples have explanations that follow an equals sign = and are enclosed in square brackets [ ]. Some examples separate the two or more sentences or phrases with an equals sign, to show that they are different ways of saying the same thing. Words that are shown in parentheses ( ) can be included or omitted without changing the basic meaning of the example. A slash / is used between words in an example when either of the words can be used in the same place in that example. (Words separated by slashes do not always have the same meaning.)

For examples of all of these features, see the Examples section of Using the Dictionary on pp. 14a-15a of the dictionary.

Boldface Phrases in Examples

Some verbal illustrations include a common phrase in boldface italic type (for example, "She tried to teach her dog to *play dead*"). The phrase usually appears at the entry for its most important word. If there is more than one important word (e.g., *play* and *dead*), the phrase can appear at the entries for one or both of the important words in the phrase (in this case, at both ¹**play** and ¹**dead**). Many of these boldface italic phrases have explanations that follow an equals sign and are enclosed by square brackets (e.g., "[=to lie on its back and pretend to be dead]"). Boldface italic phrases that are easy to understand have no glosses.

"— + adverb/preposition" Notes

Many entries in the dictionary include notes that show the common ways in which the entry word is used with other words (these are often called *collocations*). For example, when a word tends to be followed by an infinitive form of a verb, it may have this label before its examples: "— often followed by *to + verb*." When a word, such as *instruct*, tends to be used in passive constructions, the note "— often used as *(be) instructed*" may be used. If a word is often followed by a particular adverb or preposition, this is commonly indicated at entries; for example, the entry for **ask** has the note "— often + *about*."

See p. 14a of the dictionary for examples of collocations and other common word groups.

Plural Forms of Nouns

When one or more of a noun's senses can be plural, the noun's plural form (labeled "*pl*") is shown in boldface letters at the beginning of the entry. Often just the last part of the plural form is shown. For example, at **hotel**, the plural form *hotels* is shown in the dictionary by the ending **–tels**, and at **alumnus** the irregular plural form *alumni* is shown by the ending **–ni**. When the plural form of a compound noun is shown, a special symbol ~ is used to represent the first word or words of the noun; at **flower bed**, for example, the plural form *flower beds* is shown as ~ **beds**.

For spelling rules about how most noun plurals are formed, see Spelling Rules on p. 1965 of the dictionary.

Forms and Tenses of Verbs

Every entry for a verb in this dictionary shows the verb's different forms, in this order: third-person singular, past tense, past participle (if it is different from the past tense), and present participle. When a verb is regular, only the endings are shown; for example, the entry for **divide** shows -**vides** (third-person singular), -**vided** (past tense, past participle), and -**viding** (present participle). When a verb is irregular, all its forms are written out in full; thus, the entry for **write** shows **writes** (third-person singular), **wrote** (past tense), **written** (past participle), and **writing** (present participle).

For an in-depth discussion and examples of the forms of verbs, see The English Verb System on pp. 1936-44 of the dictionary. The irregular verbs are listed on pp. 1953-56.

Comparative and Superlative Forms

Adjectives and adverbs that describe qualities that can exist in different amounts or degrees have special comparative and superlative forms. For many short adjectives and a few adverbs, *-er* is added at the end of the word to form the comparative, and *-est* is added to form the superlative. These forms are shown in boldface at the beginning of the entry. For spelling rules about how most comparatives and superlatives are formed, see Spelling Rules on p. 1965 of the dictionary.

Many other adjectives are used with the words *more, most, less,* and *least* for their comparative and superlative forms. These adjectives are given the label "[*more ~; most ~*]," which usually appears at the beginning of the entry. When the label does not apply to the entire entry, it appears only at one or more of the individual senses. When an adverb is shown at the end of the entry for an adjective that has a "[*more ~; most ~*]" label, the adverb can be used with *more, most, less,* and *least*, even though the label is not repeated.

Additional information about comparatives and superlatives can be found on pp. 17a-18a and 1949-50 of the dictionary.

"count," "noncount," "singular," and "plural" Nouns

Count nouns are nouns or noun senses that may be counted (e.g., **box**: "a box," "five boxes," etc.) and that have the label "[*count*]" in this dictionary. A few count nouns have the same form for both singular and plural uses (**deer**: "a deer," "three deer"). Noncount nouns, which have the label "[*noncount*]," are never counted and have no plural form. However, most noncount nouns may be preceded by quantity words, such as *some, more,* and *less* (**wealth**: "some wealth," "less wealth," etc.). When a noun can be used as both a count and a noncount noun, it is sometimes given the label "[*count, noncount*]."

Nouns or noun senses with the label "[*singular*]" have no plural form and never follow numbers or quantity words. Nouns or noun senses with the label "[*plural*]" always take a plural form of a verb.

Nouns are discussed further on pp. 1927-28 of the dictionary.

Transitive and Intransitive Verbs

A transitive verb always has a direct object (a noun, pronoun, or noun phrase that follows the verb and names the person or thing that receives the action of the verb). An intransitive verb never has an object. Sometimes one sense (or one use of a sense) of a verb is transitive and another is intransitive. In this dictionary, "[+ *obj*]" indicates that a word, sense, or use of a sense is transitive, and "[*no obj*]" indicates that a word, sense, or use of a sense is intransitive.

See p. 1941 of the dictionary for a discussion of transitive and intransitive verbs.

Regional Labels: American and British Usage

Some words and senses are common only in American English, some are common only in British English, and some are common in one (either American or British English) and also sometimes used in the other. In this dictionary, such words or senses are given the label *"US," "Brit," "chiefly US,"* or *"chiefly Brit."* The note *"called also (Brit)"* is used at the end of an entry or sense to show the British equivalent of an American word.

The Other Labels section of Using the Dictionary on pp. 18a-19a of the dictionary discusses where regional labels are placed in dictionary entries.

Subject, Status, and Register Labels

Subject labels in the dictionary, such as *"baseball," "law," "medical," "politics," "physics,"* and *"sports,"* tell you what subject a particular word or sense relates to. The status labels *"slang," "offensive," "obscene,"* and *"impolite"* tell you how a word is judged by many English speakers. Register labels, including *"informal," "formal," "literary," "old-fashioned," "humorous," "technical,"* and *"disapproving,"* describe the usual social context in which a word or sense is used.

Explanations for each label are given in the Labels Used in This Dictionary section on p. 21a of the dictionary. The Other Labels section of Using the Dictionary on pp. 18a-19a discusses where regional labels are placed in entries.

"especially," "specifically," "broadly," and "also" Labels

Some entries in this dictionary include labels that divide a sense into two definitions. The labels *"especially"* and *"specifically"* introduce a definition that is more specific than the definition that comes before it. The label *"broadly"* introduces a definition that is more general than the one that comes before it. The label *"also"* is used for a definition that is closely related to the one that it follows. So, for example, sense 5 of **dense** is "difficult to understand; *especially* : hard to read," which means that *dense* is often used to describe writing that is difficult to read or understand.

"always used . . . ," "not used . . . ," etc. Labels

At many dictionary entries, a note in italics describes how the word, or one of its senses, is used with other parts of speech. These notes include *"always used before a noun," "not used before a noun," "always used after a noun,"* and *"always followed by an adverb or preposition."*

Figurative Use

The notes "sometimes used figuratively" and "often used figuratively" indicate that the entry word is commonly used with a meaning that isn't literal. For example, a *pipeline* is defined literally as "a line of connected pipes that are used for carrying liquids and gases over a long distance," but figuratively, a pipeline can be a way to move almost anything (such as information or weapons) from one place or person to another.

"see" and "see also" Cross-References

A "see" cross-reference tells you that more information about an entry word can be found at another entry. For example, [1]**short** includes the note "*a short fuse* see [2]FUSE," which tells you that the phrase *a short fuse* is defined at [2]**fuse**. A cross-reference note that begins with "see also" usually points to another entry where a related word or phrase is defined. For example, [1]**kid** includes the note "— see also KID GLOVES."

For more examples of "see" and "see also" cross-references, see pp. 19a-20a of the dictionary.

"compare" Cross-References

Some entries in the dictionary include a "compare" note. "Compare" notes are placed at the entries for words that are similar or that may be confused with each other; for example, **macrocosm** has the note "— compare MICROCOSM" at its entry. A "compare" note is also included at the end of each entry when two or more homographs represent the same part of speech; for example, since there are two noun entries for the word *skate*, [1]**skate** has the note "— compare [3]SKATE," and [3]**skate** has the note "— compare [1]SKATE."

Synonym Paragraphs

Some entries (such as **plentiful**) include a discussion of several synonyms for the headword. Such discussions are enclosed in a box and usually placed at the end of the entry. Other entries include a note indicating that a synonym paragraph at another entry includes a discussion of the entry word. For example, the entry for **abundant** includes the note "*synonyms* see PLENTIFUL," which indicates that *abundant* is discussed in the synonym paragraph at **plentiful**.

Phrases Discussed in ✧ Notes

In the dictionary, the symbol ✧ is used to introduce notes that explain the origins of a word (as at the entry for **Scrooge**) or provide other kinds of information. At many entries, the meaning of a boldface phrase is discussed in a sentence that begins with this symbol.

Usage Paragraphs

There is sometimes confusion or disagreement among English speakers about how a word is used or should be used. When this is the case, a usage paragraph is often included at the word's entry in order to discuss the issue (as at the entry **ain't**). Usage paragraphs are also sometimes included at an entry in order to give additional grammatical information about the use of a word. Such discussions are enclosed in a box and placed at the individual sense that the issue relates to.

Illustrations

The dictionary contains more than 1,000 original illustrations, illustrating more than 1,300 American and British terms. Many of these drawings are presented in groups showing related elements, objects, plants, animals, etc.

Geographical Names

Each entry in the Geographical Names section of the dictionary includes a brief definition that gives a general idea of the place that the name refers to. Some of the geographical entries include undefined entries for a noun or adjective that is related to the geographical name; for example, the entry for **Afghanistan** includes the undefined words **Afghan** and **Afghani**.

Grammar

An in-depth review of English grammar is provided beginning on p. 1927 of the dictionary.

Contractions

English speakers often shorten (or *contract*) the words *have*, *has*, *had*, *is*, *am*, *are*, *will*, *would*, and *not* in speech and informal writing. Certain other words also have contracted forms. These common contractions are discussed on p. 1957 of the dictionary.

Prefixes and Suffixes

Prefixes are added to the beginnings of words to change their meaning; suffixes are added to the ends of words. Each prefix and suffix has its own entry in the dictionary. See pp. 1958-59 for a list of common prefixes and suffixes.

English Word Roots

Most words in English are formed from Greek or Latin root words. Learners who know the meanings of these roots will be able to better understand and remember the meaning of many English words. A list of common Greek and Latin roots, with English words that are based on them, appears on pp. 1960-61 of the dictionary.

Spelling Rules

Many of the rules that govern English spelling are listed on pp. 1965-67 of the dictionary. This section also includes a list of words that are often misspelled by native English speakers, and discusses the differences between American and British spelling.

The Spelling of Different Sounds in English

For almost every sound that is heard in English, there is more than one way that the sound is written. For example, the /r/ sound is represented as *r* in the word *red*, as *rh* in *rhyme*, as *rr* in *arrive*, and as *wr* in *write*. A table showing the most common ways that individual sounds are spelled in English is provided on pp. 1968-69 of the dictionary.

Style: Punctuation

Punctuation is discussed in the Handbook of Style on pp. 1970-73 of the dictionary.

Style: Capitals and Italics

The uses of capital letters and italic type are discussed in the Handbook of Style on pp. 1974-76 of the dictionary.

Common First Names

Common first names and nicknames in four English-speaking countries are listed on pp. 1977-78 of the dictionary.

Money

The money of four English-speaking countries is described on p. 1979 of the dictionary.

Numbers

A guide to writing and saying different types of numbers is provided on pp. 1980-81 of the dictionary.

Weights and Measures

The standard measures for weight, volume, length, and area in the metric, U.S., and British systems are shown on pp. 1982-83 of the dictionary.

Dates

A guide to the different ways of writing and saying dates is provided on p. 1984 of the dictionary.

Holidays

The main holidays in four English-speaking countries are listed on p. 1985 of the dictionary.

Envelope Addresses

The different ways that envelope addresses are written in four English-speaking countries are discussed on pp. 1986-87 of the dictionary.

E-mail, Letters, Résumés, and Memos

A guide to writing several kinds of documents is provided on pp. 1989-93 of the dictionary.

ALPHABETICAL ORDER

1. ebony, e-book, eco-, E. coli, -ed **2.** Gothic, go-to, GPS, grab bag, grabby **3.** Kabuki, kick up, kickoff, kick-start, kid-glove **4.** o'clock, Oct., octave, OD, odd couple

All four questions require learners to ignore spaces and punctuation marks in alphabetizing. In question 3, since the phrasal verb *kick up* is part of the main entry for *kick*, *kick up* is therefore entered before *kickoff*.

GUIDEWORDS

1. actual, adder **2.** alternative, alpha **3.** arm

In question 1, *actual* would be entered before *actually*, and *adder* would follow *add*. In question 2, *alpha* would be entered before *alpha and omega*, and *alternative* would follow *alternating current*. In question 3, *arm* would follow *arithmetic*.

MOST COMMON WORDS

1. although, through, tough, thorough, cough, enough

2. Not underlined: differ, teens. Idiom: takes a back seat

Question 2: When a word can be used as different parts of speech (for example, as a noun and a verb), when it has different forms (plural, verb tenses, etc.), or when its entry includes undefined words at the end, all of these parts of speech, forms, and undefined words together are counted as only one of the 3,000 words in Merriam-Webster's list. So, for example, the plural *adults* and the participle *reading* in this exercise are included in the most common words, because **adult** and **read** are underlined in blue in the dictionary. The idiom *take a back seat* is defined at the main entry **backseat**.

HOMOGRAPHS

A. 1. 1 **2.** 2 **3.** 3 **4.** 2 **5.** 3 **6.** 1 **7.** 3 **8.** 2 **9.** 4

B. 1. 2 (verb) **2.** 2 (verb) **3.** 2 (verb) **4.** 3 (noun) **5.** 3 (noun) **6.** 2 (verb) **7.** 2 (verb) **8.** 3 (adjective) **9.** 1 (adverb) **10.** 2 (preposition)

COMPOUNDS

A. 1. floss **2.** people **3.** driver **4.** ground **5.** Riley **6.** reaction **7.** floor **8.** towel **9.** on **10.** time

B. 1. saving **2.** breathing **3.** forming **4.** drawn **5.** breasted **6.** rent **7.** readable **8.** aged **9.** racking **10.** fashioned

C. 1. con artist **2.** old-fashioned **3.** singer-songwriter **4.** chalkboard **5.** (correct) **6.** pistol-whip **7.** witch hazel **8.** (correct) **9.** guinea pig **10.** half-moon **11.** pitch-black **12.** dry-clean **13.** chin-up **14.** jerry-rigged **15.** court-martial

Many compounds are not entered in the dictionary; new compounds are often invented by writers for a single use. However, each of the compounds in these questions has its own main entry in the dictionary.

ABBREVIATIONS

A. 1. female, feminine, forte **2.** gram **3.** male, married, meter, mile **4.** page, per, pence, penny

B. 1. centimeter **2.** emergency room **3.** kilometer **4.** railroad, rural route

C. 1. apartment, aptitude **2.** column **3.** dozen **4.** gallon

D. 1. antilock braking system **2.** barbecue **3.** date of birth **4.** high-occupancy vehicle

E. 1. estimated time of arrival **2.** intensive care unit **3.** personal identification number **4.** research and development

Part E: In question 4, the learner who looks up *R & D* should remember that it is alphabetized in the dictionary as if it were spelled out as *randd*.

TRADEMARKS

1. (correct) **2.** Band-Aid **3.** Dumpster **4.** Frisbee **5.** (correct) **6.** Jet Ski **7.** Kleenex **8.** Ping-Pong **9.** Popsicle **10.** Rollerblade

Since *snooker* and *cribbage* are not the names of companies or their exclusive products, they are not trademarks or brand names.

IDIOMS

1. i (at **¹pound**) **2.** d (at **⁴lie**) **3.** b (at **¹rub**) **4.** e (at **²loose**) **5.** g (at **²wrap**) **6.** j (at **¹lunch**) **7.** h (at **¹net**) **8.** a (at **¹fish**) **9.** f (at **¹man**) **10.** c (at **²crack**)

There is often more than one entry at which a particular idiom might be entered. The headwords where these idioms are actually entered are shown here in parentheses, with their homograph numbers.

PHRASAL VERBS

1. g **2.** i **3.** m **4.** e **5.** t **6.** p **7.** o **8.** a **9.** h
10. r **11.** d **12.** f **13.** s **14.** b **15.** j **16.** q
17. c **18.** l **19.** n **20.** k

Most of the phrasal verbs listed in the exercise have only one sense, but some have more. For example, *give in* has two senses; sense 1, the intransitive sense, is the one required here.

UNDEFINED WORDS

1. alert **2.** geography **3.** rancor **4.** reactionary
5. bleak **6.** mayor **7.** embargo **8.** twenty
9. archaeology **10.** rapacious **11.** tassel
12. thug **13.** sabbatical **14.** shortsighted
15. languor

The boldface words at the end of an entry do not have definitions, but their meanings should be easy to determine. In the dictionary, the first sense of the suffix **-ly** is defined as "in a (specified) manner," so the answer to question 1 is "in an alert manner." Since ¹**alert** is defined as "able to think clearly and to notice things," the definition of **alertly** would be "able to think clearly and to notice things" + "in an alert manner," or "in a manner in which someone or something is able to think clearly and to notice things."

PRONUNCIATIONS

A. 1. rein, reign, rain **2.** peak, peek, pique

B. 1. jacket **2.** paddle **3.** fiction **4.** highway
5. method

C. 1. h **2.** p,s **3.** p **4.** t **5.** ch

Part A: In question 1, *rein*, *reign*, and *rain* are all pronounced /ˈreɪn/. *Range* is instead pronounced /ˈreɪndʒ/, and *rang* is pronounced /ˈræŋ/. (The pronunciation for *rang* can be found at ³**ring**.) In question 2, *peak*, *peek*, and *pique* are all pronounced /ˈpiːk/, while *pike* is pronounced /ˈpaɪk/ and *pick* is pronounced /ˈpɪk/.

Part B: To answer these questions, learners need to be (or to become) familiar with the IPA. For example, in question 1, the learner can begin by looking up the /dʒ/ symbol in the list of IPA symbols (p. 22a or p. 1994) and see that /dʒ/ is usually represented at the beginning of an English word by the letter *j*. By looking up each symbol in the pronunciation, he or she will soon find the word in the dictionary that contains the same symbols.

VARIANT SPELLINGS

1. amoeba **2.** boatswain **3.** cauldron **4.** jinni
5. phyllo **6.** gibe **7.** caftan **8.** medevac
9. nosy **10.** pricey **11.** mannikin **12.** old
13. man-sized **14.** rumba **15.** rock and roll

The Spelling section of Using the Dictionary on pp. 12a-13a gives examples of how variants are treated in the dictionary.

DEFINITIONS: SENSES

1. g **2.** d **3.** h **4.** e **5.** b **6.** a **7.** o **8.** s **9.** f
10. r **11.** c **12.** n **13.** l **14.** m **15.** t **16.** i
17. k **18.** j **19.** p **20.** q

For each question, the learner is asked to identify sense 2 of a homograph. This requires the learner to look up each word, which is the only way to be sure of the meaning of sense 2. The "basic meanings" that are listed in the column on the right are short versions of their dictionary definitions.

DEFINITIONS: SUBSENSES

1. 1a **2.** 1b **3.** 8a **4.** 5c **5.** 2a **6.** 2b **7.** 3a
8. 2a **9.** 5b **10.** 2b

Most of the phrases that are used in questions 1-10 are highlighted in examples in the dictionary. To find the correct subsenses, learners must look for the highlighted phrases within the correct dictionary entry. For example, at ¹**date**, the boldface italic example "*set a date*" is included at sense 1a; thus, the answer is 1a.

TYPES OF DEFINITIONS

1. — **2.** ✧ (at ²**answer**) **3.** ✧ (at ¹**game**)
4. : **5.** — **6.** — **7.** ✧ (at ²**turn**)
8. ✧ (at ²**jump**) **9.** — **10.** :

The Definitions section of Using the Dictionary on p. 13a gives examples of the different types of definitions in the dictionary.

SYNONYMS AND ANTONYMS

A. 1. B and B **2.** pager **3.** drainpipe
4. thighbone **5.** chickpea **6.** little finger
7. navel **8.** loser **9.** emptiness **10.** flip-flop

B. 1. defeat **2.** nonstandard **3.** criminalize
4. miss **5.** stiff

Part A: The answers for questions 1-4 are entered in "*called also*" notes at the end of their entries of individual senses. The answers for questions 5, 6, 7, and 10 appear in small capital letters. The answers for questions 8 and 9 appear in square brackets within example phrases or sentences.

EXAMPLE SENTENCES AND PHRASES

A. 1. We have been studying ancient Greek mythology. **2.** They ribbed him about/over his silly outfit. **3.** She babysits their kids on Saturday nights. **4.** He was wearing (a pair of) jeans. **5.** a rusty old car

B. 1. watch **2.** us **3.** Sundays **4.** blew **5.** children **6.** on **7.** different, cultural **8.** murder **9.** police **10.** poor **11.** hand **12.** placed **13.** busy **14.** ability **15.** copies **16.** waste **17.** comments **18.** storm **19.** cat **20.** cheered **21.** gusts **22.** curtains **23.** flavor **24.** trees **25.** restaurant **26.** project **27.** plant **28.** pivoted, changed **29.** can, help, build **30.** minerals

BOLDFACE PHRASES IN EXAMPLES

A. 1. (at ²**jab**) criticized **2.** (at ¹**slope**) go skiing **3.** (at ¹**trouble**) making the effort **4.** (at ¹**face**) in the world **5.** (at **idea**) understand **6.** (at **obeisance**) showed or expressed great respect **7.** (at **mad**, ²**raving**, and ²**stark**) completely insane **8.** (at ¹**hate** and ¹**mail**) extremely angry letters, e-mail, etc. **9.** (at ³**deal**) make the agreement official **10.** (at ¹**brief**) a few words

B. 1. (at **rock bottom**) reached the lowest point they can reach **2.** (at ¹**voice**) speak quietly **3.** mess, predicament **4.** (at ¹**stand**) hate **5.** (at ¹**man**) the human race in modern times **6.** (at **mile**) very fast **7.** (at **glowing**) in a very enthusiastic way **8.** (at ¹**grab**) sit down **9.** volume **10.** not a pleasant experience

This answer key shows where particular phrases are treated in the dictionary. For most of the answers, the appropriate headword and homograph number are shown in parentheses. When the boldface phrase has only one important word, the headword is not shown.

"— + ADVERB/PREPOSITION"

A. 1. of **2.** up **3.** to **4.** of **5.** to **6.** on **7.** for **8.** on **9.** for **10.** for

B. 1. on **2.** (correct) **3.** to **4.** out **5.** back

PLURAL FORMS OF NOUNS

1. attorneys at law **2.** children **3.** criteria **4.** feet **5.** heroes **6.** moose **7.** mice

8. silos **9.** wives **10.** analyses

The questions in this set of exercises mainly deal with nouns with irregular plurals. Some of these plural forms are discussed in the Spelling Rules section (p. 1965); however, all can be found simply by looking up their singular forms in the dictionary.

1. *Attorney at law* forms its plural by adding *-s* to *attorney* rather than to *law*.

2. *Children* is an irregular plural that is formed in its own unique way.

3. *Criterion* is one of a very few nouns that become plural by changing their *-ion* endings to *-ia*.

4. *Foot* forms its plural in a completely irregular way.

5. *Hero* is one of the nouns that end in an *-o* following a consonant and form their plurals by adding *–es*.

6. *Moose*, like some other animal names, does not change its spelling in its plural form.

7. *Mouse* forms its plural in a completely irregular way.

8. *Silo*, like *hero*, ends in an *-o* that follows a consonant, but forms its plural by simply adding *-s*.

9. *Wife* is one of the few nouns that forms its plural by changing the ending *-fe* to *-ves*.

10. As a word of Greek origin that ends in *–is*, *analysis* forms its plural by changing *-is* to *-es*.

FORMS AND TENSES OF VERBS

1. fell, fallen, falling **2.** decided, decided, deciding **3.** forgave, forgiven, forgiving **4.** shed, shed, shedding **5.** swam, swum, swimming

The list of Irregular Verbs on pp. 1953-56 of the dictionary shows the infinitive, past, and past participle forms of all the common irregular verbs. However, all the dictionary's individual entries for verbs, both regular and irregular, show the verb's third-person singular, past tense, past participle (if it is different from the past tense), and present participle forms. Thus, a learner may find the main part of the dictionary more helpful than the Irregular Verbs list for answering the questions in this section.

For the verbs in questions 1, 3, and 5, each of the three forms is written out at the main entry in the dictionary. For questions 2 and 4, the past and past participle are the same: *decided* is both the past and the past participle of *decide* ("I decided to go," "I have decided to go"), and *shed* is both the past and the past participle of *shed* ("It shed its skin," "It had shed its skin"). Thus, only the past form is written out at these verbs' entries.

COMPARATIVE AND SUPERLATIVE FORMS

1. neater, neatest **2.** braver, bravest
3. faster, fastest **4.** more radiant, most radiant
5. heavier, heaviest **6.** more representative, most representative **7.** more jaded, most jaded
8. rawer, rawest **9.** more just, most just
10. more heavily, most heavily **11.** freer, freest
12. funner, funnest **13.** better; best
14. more idealistic, most idealistic
15. hollower, hollowest

The spelling rules for how to form the comparative (-*er*) and superlative (-*est*) forms of adjectives are discussed on p. 1965 of the dictionary.

For *brave* and *free* (questions 2 and 11), the learner must remember to remove the final -*e* before adding -*er* or -*est* to the end of each adjective. For *heavy* (question 5), the final -*y* follows a consonant and must be changed to *i* before adding -*er* or -*est*. For *fun* (question 12), a one-syllable word that ends with a consonant after a single vowel, the final consonant must be doubled before -*er* or -*est* is added.

"COUNT," "NONCOUNT," "SINGULAR," AND "PLURAL" NOUNS

A. All except 1, 3, and 4 are noncount.

B. 1. sense 2 a and b **2.** sense 2 **3.** sense 1b
4. all senses **5.** all senses

C. 1. singular **2.** usually singular **3.** singular
4. usually singular **5.** singular

TRANSITIVE AND INTRANSITIVE VERBS

A. 1. salary **2.** water **3.** wound **4.** people
5. blocks

B. Nos. 4, 6, 7, and 8 are always intransitive.

C. 1. 2, (no object) **2.** 1, roommate
3. 1d, (no object) **4.** 2, ability **5.** 4b, point

Part A: In question 1, the first transitive ([+ *obj*]) example is "She *earns* a good salary";

the direct object of *earns* is *salary*. In question 2, the first transitive example is "She *fears* [=(more commonly) *is afraid of*] the water"; *water* is the direct object of *fears*. In question 3, the first transitive example, at sense 2, is "The ointment will help *heal* the wound"; *wound* is the direct object of *heal*. In question 4, the first transitive example is "If you're sick you should stay home to avoid *infecting* other people in the office"; *people* is the direct object of *infecting*. In question 5, the first transitive example is "She *joined* [=*fastened*] the blocks of wood (together) with glue"; *blocks* is the direct object of *joined*.

REGIONAL LABELS: AMERICAN AND BRITISH USAGE

A. 1. out tray **2.** maize **3.** agony column
4. dustcart **5.** drawing pin **6.** loss adjuster
7. action replay **8.** paraffin **9.** letter box, postbox **10.** porridge

B. 1. hood **2.** sedan **3.** detour **4.** period
5. lineup **6.** diaper **7.** solitaire **8.** backpack
9. wrench **10.** calling card

Part A: Each question can be answered by looking up the American word in the dictionary and finding the "called also (*Brit*)" note at the end of the entry or the end of an individual sense.

Part B: All of these British words are defined in the dictionary by their American synonyms, which are shown in small capital letters. When the entry for the British word includes several senses, the correct sense has the label "*Brit*" (or, for question 8, "*chiefly Brit*").

SUBJECT, STATUS, AND REGISTER LABELS

A. 1. a **2.** e **3.** d **4.** b **5.** c

B. 1. c **2.** d **3.** a **4.** b **5.** b, e **6.** a, h **7.** a, h
8. g **9.** a, h **10.** g

"ESPECIALLY," "SPECIFICALLY," "BROADLY," AND "ALSO" LABELS

1. absent or missing **2.** a wild animal that is large, dangerous, or unusual **3.** a shallow bowl **4.** clothing of this color **5.** a person born or living in the eastern U.S. **6.** job **7.** the film that has such an image **8.** a bacterium that causes disease **9.** a young rabbit **10.** the plant that produces this vegetable **11.** the Olympics **12.** a fabric that is woven or knit **13.** computer equipment **14.** a member of one of these groups from the U.S. **15.** the act of making such statements

"ALWAYS USED . . . ," "NOT USED . . . ," ETC. LABELS

1. correct **2.** correct **3.** incorrect **4.** incorrect **5.** correct **6.** incorrect **7.** correct **8.** incorrect **9.** correct **10.** incorrect **11.** incorrect **12.** incorrect **13.** correct **14.** incorrect **15.** incorrect

For each word in the questions, the note given at the appropriate senses is shown here. For each of the incorrect sentences, the corrected form is shown.

1. ¹**absent**—sense 3—*always used before a noun*

2. ²**adult**—sense 1—*always used before a noun*

3. **deserving**—sense 2—*not used before a noun*. The correct form: The dinner and entertainment were deserving *of* praise.

4. **glad**—senses 1 and 2—*not used before a noun*. Possible correct forms: A clerk was glad to answer all their questions. *or* A clerk gladly answered all their questions. *or* A happy clerk answered all their questions.

5. **hungry**—sense 2—*not used before a noun*

6. **apiece**—*always used after a noun*. The correct form: The tickets cost ten dollars apiece.

7. **galore**—*always used after a noun*

8. ³**elect**—*always used after a noun*. The correct form: The president-elect was choosing his advisers.

9. ²**enough**—*always used after an adjective, adverb, or verb*

10. **aplenty**—*always used after a noun*. The correct form: There were peaches aplenty hanging from the tree.

11. **glide**—*always followed by an adverb or preposition*. The correct form: Three skiers were gliding *down* the slope.

12. ¹**knock**—sense 2—*always followed by an adverb, adjective, or preposition*. The correct form: The wind knocked him backwards. (This example uses sense 2, which is a transitive "[+ *obj*]" sense. There should be no preposition (e.g., *on*) between the verb (*knocked*) and the direct object (*him*).)

13. ¹**march**—sense 1b—*always followed by an adverb or preposition*

14. **modern-day**—*always used before a noun*. The correct form: He's a modern-day saint.

15. ²**parade**—sense 1—*always followed by an adverb or preposition*. The correct form: The protesters paraded *in front of/past* City Hall shouting slogans.

FIGURATIVE USE

A. 1. allergic to hard work **2.** bejeweled skyline **3.** gatekeepers of knowledge **4.** key to his heart **5.** spiritually nourishing

B. 1. prologue **2.** big leagues **3.** behind **4.** navigable **5.** obituary

Part B uses the figurative senses of the words given in the list. Here are the literal definitions that appear before the "*sometimes/often/usually used figuratively*" labels:

1. **prologue** : an introduction to a book, play, etc.

2. **big leagues** : the two main U.S. baseball leagues

3. ¹**behind 1b** : in the place that someone is going away from

4. **navigable** : deep and wide enough for boats and ships to travel on or through

5. **obituary** : an article in a newspaper about the life of someone who has died recently

"SEE" AND "SEE ALSO" CROSS-REFERENCES

1. first baseman, second baseman, third baseman **2.** milk of magnesia **3.** breadbasket, handbasket, wastebasket **4.** cowboy hat, hard hat, old hat, top hat **5.** homeowner, landowner **6.** credibility gap, generation gap **7.** sour grapes **8.** costume jewelry **9.** disc jockey **10.** powder keg

All of the entries in questions 3-10 include "*see also*" cross-references, while questions 1 and 2 have "*see*" cross-references. The "*see also*" cross-references at questions 3-10 direct dictionary users to related entries. "The "*see*" cross-references direct users to entries where information about the word can be found. In question 1, the entry **baseman** includes a "*see*" cross-reference to the entries **first baseman**, **second baseman**, and **third baseman**. The "*see*" cross-reference is used instead of a definition because *baseman* is never used alone. The same is true in question 2: *Magnesia* is never used except in the term *milk of magnesia*, so **magnesia** has a *"see"* cross-reference to **milk of magnesia** instead of a definition.

"COMPARE" CROSS-REFERENCES

1. maternal **2** full-size, king-size, twin-size **3.** ²peaked **4.** diameter **5.** nationalism **6.** id, superego **7.** hallmark **8.** oar **9.** full moon, new moon **10.** instrument panel

Examples of the different types of *"compare"* cross-references are shown on p. 20a of the dictionary.

SYNONYM PARAGRAPHS

1. decomposing *or* rotting **2.** impair **3.** rules **4.** values *or* cherishes **5.** power **6.** ancient **7.** price **8.** fear **9.** dank **10.** lethal

Learners can look up the italic word in the dictionary, and that entry will either contain a synonym paragraph or a note saying where the paragraph is entered.

1. At ¹**decay**, the synonym paragraph states that *decomposing* and *rotting* relate to the breaking down of something that is dead, while *decaying* relates to a general slow change from a state of strength or perfection.

2. At **injure**, the synonym paragraph states that *impair* suggests that something has been made weaker or worse, while *injure* is usually used when the body of a person or animal has been harmed.

3. At **law**, the synonym paragraph states that *rule* does not involve an official government, while *law* is made by a government and is something that people under the control of the government must obey.

4. At **appreciate**, the synonym paragraph states that *prize* is used when you are very proud of something you have or own, *value* describes something that is worth a lot because of what it is, and *cherish* describes a very strong love for someone or something.

5. At ¹**power**, the synonym paragraph states that *dominion* is used to stress the greatest or highest power or authority, while *power* is a more general term that suggests the ability to influence things.

6. At ¹**old**, the synonym paragraph states that *ancient* refers to things that happened or existed in the very distant past, while *antique* refers to objects that have been kept from the past and that are often valuable.

7. At ¹**price**, the paragraph states that *price* refers to how much money is asked for goods, while *charge* refers to the amount of money that you pay for a service.

8. At ¹**fear**, the paragraph states that *fear* suggests an emotional state that continues, while *alarm* suggests a strong emotion caused by an unexpected or immediate danger.

9. At **moist**, the paragraph states that *dank* is used to refer to a cold and unpleasant wetness that may make people sick, while *moist* usually refers to a pleasant or desirable slight wetness.

10. At ¹**deadly**, the paragraph states that *lethal* is used to refer to something like a poison that is used to destroy life, while *deadly* is used to describe something that is very dangerous and able to cause death.

PHRASES DISCUSSED IN ◇ NOTES

1. b (at **aisle**) **2.** c (at ¹**flavor**) **3.** a (at **knell**) **4.** a (at **grain**) **5.** c (at **proportion**) **6.** a (at ¹**chink**) **7.** c **8.** b (at ¹**class**) **9.** b (at ¹**collect**) **10.** a (at **ice water**)

To show where each idiom can be found in the dictionary, the appropriate headwords with their homograph numbers are included here in parentheses.

USAGE PARAGRAPHS

1. that **2.** be allowed, be permitted **3.** noncount **4.** when *neither* is followed by *of* **5.** to **6.** singular **7.** haven't got, hasn't got **8.** What's the matter? **9.** Native American **10.** toward someone or something

This section encourages learners to find where the usage paragraphs are entered in the dictionary. For question 1, the paragraph is entered at ¹**this**. For question 2, the usage paragraph is at **let**. For question 7, the usage paragraph follows the definition of **have got**, which appears at the entry **have**. For question 8, the usage paragraph appears at **matter**. For question 9, the paragraph appears at **Native American**. For question 10, the paragraph appears at **take**.

ILLUSTRATIONS

A. 1. cylinder **2.** sphere **3.** cube **4.** rectangle
5. square

B. 1. golf ball, cricket ball, softball, volleyball,
basketball **2.** mouse, squirrel, woodchuck,
beaver, porcupine **3.** violin, viola, cello, double
bass, harp

C. 1. camisole, half slip, briefs **2.** sarong,
pantyhose, pajamas, tights **3.** vest, sport coat,
suspenders

GEOGRAPHICAL NAMES

1. Filipino **2.** Scotland **3.** a Mexican island
4. Côte d'Ivoire **5.** Jordan and Israel
6. a volcano in Hawaii **7.** South America
8. China and the Mediterranean Sea
9. salt water **10.** Rangoon **11.** northern Africa
12. the Sea of Marmara and the Black Sea
13. Spain **14.** an independent country
15. Istanbul **16.** Indonesia and East Timor
17. Egypt and Greece **18.** France **19.** Tanzania
20. France and Italy

GRAMMAR

A. 1. linking verb **2.** gerund **3.** demonstrative
pronoun **4.** adverb **5.** indefinite pronoun
6. demonstrative adjective **7.** modal verb
8. interrogative adverb **9.** coordinating
conjunction **10.** predicate adjective

B. 1. We don't have <u>much/any</u> milk, but there
are <u>some</u> doughnuts. **2.** She didn't <u>go</u> home
after the movie, and she still <u>hasn't</u> called.
3. They <u>enjoyed</u> seeing <u>California</u>, but they
didn't <u>enjoy</u> (the) American food. **4.** When he
<u>was</u> young, he <u>read</u> about dinosaurs all the
time. **5.** He <u>has</u> taken the car somewhere; I
don't <u>know</u> when he will be back. **6.** The pasta
would be better if it <u>had</u> more salt. **7.** <u>The</u> sun
shined brightly in <u>the</u> morning, but <u>the</u> sky
became cloudy in <u>the</u> afternoon. **8.** You aren't
going to work today, <u>are you</u>? **9.** She showed
me her <u>beautiful green BMW sports car</u>.
10. He <u>loves</u> to go to nightclubs, but I always
<u>prefer</u> to stay home.

C. 1. Alex is taking the test today, and his
brother will take the same one next spring.
2. Some short films will be shown by us first,
and then the CEO will give the awards.
3. His parents had prepared the dinner, and
dessert was brought by his sister. **4.** Many
people prefer big department stores, but
smaller shops are preferred by others.

5. The Australians beat the Japanese team, but
the United States was defeated by Spain.

The grammar terms being tested in this section
are generally advanced and can be challenging
for many learners. Learners should be
encouraged to study and use the dictionary's
English Grammar Review while completing this
section.

CONTRACTIONS

A. 1. you'd / I'd have (*or* I would've) **2.** They're
/ we'll **3.** hadn't / we'd **4.** doesn't / couldn't
5. he'd / wasn't

B. 1. was not / you have **2.** would not / had
not **3.** has not / is not **4.** should have / was
not **5.** should not / you are **6.** do not know /
Mom will **7.** He has / got to / them **8.** Let me /
you are / going to **9.** There is / that is / sort of
10. We would / kind of

PREFIXES AND SUFFIXES

A. 1. antibacterial **2.** coauthor **3.** disagreeable
4. inconsistent **5.** international **6.** misjudge
7. nonalcoholic **8.** defrost **9.** subconscious
10. unconstitutional

B. 1. upward **2.** goodness **3.** peaceful
4. talkative **5.** personal **6.** slowly **7.** poisonous
8. childless **9.** Marxism **10.** flirtation

C. 1. prepay **2.** substandard **3.** overfill
4. postnatal **5.** unilateral **6.** nonviolent
7. transcontinental **8.** misstate
9. counterproductive **10.** interplanetary

When a prefix or suffix and a base word are
correctly combined, the word they form is
entered in the dictionary. Many words with
added suffixes appear only as undefined terms.

ENGLISH WORD ROOTS

1. arm (weapon) **2.** aud (hearing) **3.** bio (life),
graph (write) **4.** dic (speak) **5.** fid (faith)
6. metr (measure) **7.** pot (power)
8. nov (new) **9.** tele (distant), scop (look, view)
10. san (health)

SPELLING RULES

A. 1. accommodate **2.** category **3.** (correct)
4. inoculate **5.** occurred

B. 1. meager **2.** estrogen **3.** realize **4.** traveled
5. fervor

C. 1. sashes **2.** crazier **3.** confesses **4.** thieves
5. gladder **6.** sews **7.** sharper **8.** CEOs

9. bases **10**. donkeys **11**. sees **12**. lorries **13**. brunches **14**. savvier **15**. fades

Part A: These words are all included in the list titled Words Often Misspelled (p. 1966).

Part B: The American vs. British Spelling section (p. 1967) discusses the ways that the two types of English differ.

1. The US spelling *meager* and the British spelling *meagre* is an example of the *-er/-re* difference that is seen at the ends of many words.

2. The US *estrogen* and the British *oestrogen* is an example of the *-e-/-oe-* difference found in the spelling of many words that come from Greek.

3. The US *realize* and the British *realise* show that American words ending in *-ize* or *-yze* are often spelled *-ise* or *-yse* in British English.

4. The US *traveled* and the British *travelled* show that, in British English, the final *-l* of a verb is doubled when *-ed* or *-ing* is added at the end.

5. The US *fervor* and the British *fervour* shows that *-or-* in American words often appears as *-our-* in British words.

Part C: Here are the rules for writing the forms of the adjectives, nouns, and verbs in this section:

1. For nouns ending in *-sh*, add *-es* to form the plural.

2. For adjectives that end with a *-y* that follows a consonant, change the *-y* to *-i* before adding *-er* to form the comparative.

3. For verbs that end in *-s*, add *-es* to form the present-tense third-person singular.

4. For some nouns that end in *-f*, change the *-f* to *-ves*.

5. For one-syllable adjectives that end in a consonant that follows a single vowel, double the final consonant.

6. For most verbs, add *-s*.

7. For most adjectives, add *-er*.

8. For abbreviations written in capital letters, add *-s* or *-'s*. (See the Abbreviations section on p. 1975.)

9. For words of Greek origin ending in *-is*, replace the *-is* with *-es*.

10. For nouns ending in a *-y* that follows a vowel, add *-s*.

11. For most verbs, add *-s*.

12. For nouns ending in a *-y* that follows a consonant, change the *-y* to *-i* before adding *-es*.

13. For nouns ending in *-ch*, add *-es*.

14. For adjectives ending in a *-y* that follows a consonant, change the *-y* to *-i* before adding *-er*.

15. For most verbs, add *-s*.

THE SPELLING OF DIFFERENT SOUNDS IN ENGLISH

1. cot, bone, do **2**. famous, loud, boulder, youth, could **3**. cc, ck, cq

For question 3, learners should look at the different ways to spell the /k/ sound on p. 1968 of the dictionary, then look in the main part of the dictionary to see if any entries begin with these spellings.

STYLE: PUNCTUATION

On April 18-19, 2009, Rex's Tavern will host its second-ever charity darts tournament to benefit the Tall Oaks Boys' and Girls' Camp of Manchester.

Last year there were twenty-five competitors, and Jerome White, the owner of Rex's, says he is hoping to bring in double that number this year. The top prizes for this year's event will be a state-of-the-art GPS system and an MP3 player. These prizes will be donated by Rick Davidson of Rick's Electronics. Hats, mugs, and gift certificates will also be offered as door prizes.

"It's going to be a great time," said White. "We'll have all of our best beers on tap and an array of live performers, and it's all going to a great cause."

The winner of last year's tournament, Michael Jones, said that he is prepared to defend his title. Holding a rabbit's foot for good luck, Jones said, "It was a blast last year. I met a lot of good friends, and hopefully there'll be more people competing this year."

In addition to the entry fees, White said, two-thirds of all food and beverage sales from the tournament will be donated to Tall Oaks. Two other local businesses will help to sponsor the event: Henderson's Import Auto Sales and Martinelli's Pizza.

The entry fee is twenty dollars. White said that players will not need to pre-register for the tournament, but those who wish to enter should arrive at the tavern no later than two o'clock on April 18.

STYLE: CAPITALS AND ITALICS

Anderson's Book Shop in West Charlestown will host a signing and lecture by financial expert Suzanne Walker, author of the best-selling investment guide *Going for Broke: Speculation in a Pool of Risk,* on Saturday at 2:00 p.m.

Walker's first book, *Take the Money and Run,* was chosen by the *New York Times* as one of the notable books of 2003, and was a finalist for an award from the magazines *Fortune* and *Business Week*. *Going for Broke* has already sold 200,000 copies.

Publisher's Weekly called *Going for Broke* "a must-read for anyone who's looking to invest in the market." Cara Richardson of the *Wall Street Journal* wrote, "In this era of specialized investing and overspeculation, it's become more difficult for the amateur investor to make rational decisions about where to put his or her money. *Going for Broke* answers those questions in plain English that's a pleasure to read."

If you would like to reserve a seat for this event, please call Lori McNulty at (242) 555-2727.

COMMON FIRST NAMES

All of the following are correct: Andy, Chris, Denny, Jackie, Lou, Nicky, Pat, Robin, Sam, Sammy, Sandy, Terry

MONEY

1. b **2.** c **3.** b **4.** b **5.** a

NUMBERS

1. one million **2.** 100,000 **3.** MMIX **4.** ninety-fifth **5.** one thousand five hundred, fifteen hundred **6.** five-eighths **7.** two and a half **8.** "point one five" **9.** "zero point six five four" **10.** 1812

WEIGHTS AND MEASURES

1. metric ton **2.** liter **3.** hectare **4.** meter **5.** kilogram

DATES

1. March 4, 2005 **2.** 4 March 2005 **3.** 3/4/05 **4.** 4/3/05 **5.** 2005-03-04

HOLIDAYS

1. a **2.** c **3.** b **4.** a, c **5.** d

ENVELOPE ADDRESSES

1. The city name is missing. **2.** The postcode should be below the city name. **3.** The postcode contains no letters. **4.** The state abbreviation is missing. **5.** The zip code should have five digits.

E-MAIL, LETTERS, RÉSUMÉS, AND MEMOS

1. Very truly yours, Sincerely yours, Yours sincerely **2.** Any of the following: age, race, religion, height or weight, general health, marital status **3.** salutation, complimentary close, signature